DOG TRAINING
THE SMART WAY

DOG

TRAINING

THE SMART WAY

THE #1 COMPLETE GUIDE
FOR ANY AGE OR BREED

BEORE YOU BEGIN:
FREE BONUS GUIDES

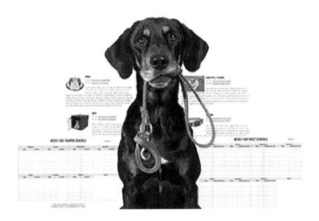

Training can be a daunting prospect and the last thing you need is to be unsure about your schedule or equipment.

To help you out during training I've put together a free bonus bundle including:

- Free Weekly Dog Training Schedule Template

- Training Equipment Guide

- Toilet Diary Template

Visit www.litomedia.com/dog-training to get yours!

TABLE OF CONTENTS

"A dog is the only thing on earth that loves you more than you love yourself."

Josh Billings

INTRODUCTION

So you got a dog, huh? High five! That big bundle of fat and fluff will be a loyal and loving companion for years to come. If you train it right, that is.

Just like children, the character of a dog is largely influenced in its early days. The sooner you begin training the easier it will be, but that doesn't mean you can't teach an old dog new tricks.

That myth has long been debunked and has absolutely no credibility whatsoever. People adopt older dogs every day and are able to take training as far as they want to go with it.

Using the proven techniques and easy to follow training drills in this book you too can raise a respectful, obedient and gentle dog.

Now, there are some bogus books out there making spurious claims such as 'train your dog in 7 days' and, let me just tell you, that is a fast track to ruining their development.

You wouldn't send a child to school for a week and consider them educated, so you shouldn't cut corners when it comes to training your dog either.

Having been around them my entire life I have learnt firsthand how invaluable it is to start a dog off right with a good training schedule and continue to maintain it going forward. This book will teach you the key techniques required for long-term success.

I use only proven and verified positive reinforcement training methods which allow you to bond with your dog through reward-based learning. There is no place for physical punishment or scolding in any form of training and you won't find it here.

Give your new friend the start they deserve by following a training schedule which has already helped plenty of dogs become healthy, happy members of the family.

Good luck and happy training,

R.Woolfe

HOW TO USE THIS BOOK

This book is your training bible. You should not merely read the words but *live* by them. There will be times when you just want to cave in and roll around on the floor with your dog but be strong, no matter how darn cute that sideways thing they do with their head is!

Here are 5 quick tips to help you get the most out of this book and give your dog the best possible start in life:

1. **Be prepared:** It's a good idea to read this book *before* you adopt so you don't end up trying to cram bits of training in here and there while running around after them once they've arrived. You can then top up your knowledge during or between sessions, too.

2. **Be strong:** I know the temptation to cave in to the cuteness and play with your new friend all day long can be overwhelming but always remember that a poorly raised dog will grow up to be a badly behaved one. By taking these steps now you are avoiding problems later down the line so bear this in mind whenever you interact with them.

3. **Be consistent**: There is nothing more confusing for a dog than inconsistent training. If you have off days or let them get away with things here and there they will struggle to learn. Stick to the schedule we will set later and be consistent in everything you do to ensure your dog learns fast and remembers forever.

4. **Be patient:** Every dog is different and some will need more work than others, so don't get frustrated if they don't pick things up right away. With good, consistent training they will learn everything they need to set them up for a long and happy life.

5. **Be nice:** My mantra when it comes to training is to focus solely on reward-based learning. Not only is this the most efficient and effective method, it is also the only morally acceptable way.

You will never build a trusting relationship with a dog by scolding or physically punishing it. Instead we will use a combination of small food treats, praise and affection to reward your dog for good behavior so you can build a strong, lasting bond.

So, now you are prepped for the task, it's time to make sure your home is too.

CHAPTER 1

DOG-PROOFING YOUR HOME

Dogs are inquisitive creatures and will likely explore places in your home that you forgot even existed. Here's a quick guide on protecting your dog and home from one and other.

Tip: The first thing you should know is that even if you wrap everything in your house in protective plastic and then coat it in Teflon twice your dog is still going to find something to gnaw at or pee on, especially if young.

Please be patient with them and remember that this is part and parcel of training a dog. There will always be a bit of collateral damage, but here's how you can limit it:

- **Tidy Up**: It seems obvious but the best thing you can do to stop your dog destroying things is to simply move them out of reach. Spend time clearing away clutter regularly and pay special attention to ensuring small things which they could swallow are completely out of reach. Having a tidy home will actually help your dog learn faster too, as there will be less visual stimulation to distract them from training.

- **Electricals**: Dogs explore with their mouths so wires and other electrical appliances pose a big threat to their wellbeing. Make sure all wires are flush to the wall and wrapped in protective sleeves. Unplugging things and turning the sockets off when not in use will also make sure your friend stays safe.

- **Plants**: If you have plants indoors or out, perform a quick check to ensure you don't have any poisonous species which he or she could ingest.

- **Chemicals & Cosmetics**: Curious dogs can often find their way into cabinets and cupboards, so it's a good idea to fit low doors with childproof latches.

- **Food**: Many human foods such as chocolate or those high in sugar or fat can be harmful to dogs, so be sure to keep these well out of reach. You should also keep your dog's food hidden as if they uncover it they could eat themselves sick.

- **Trash & Bin Bags**: Get used to cleaning up as you go along as leaving things even for a small amount of time could give your dog an opportunity to get into them and harm themselves with whatever nasty things are within.

- **Bolt Holes**: Dogs are explorers by nature so make sure you don't leave doors or windows open. If you have a cat flap keep that secure too. It's also important to go out into the yard and check for any holes in the fencing, although you should never leave them alone there anyway.

- **Ponds or Pools:** If your dog can make their way into deep water then you need to ensure they can make their way out, too. Train them to swim and climb out as soon as you are able to do so and never leave them unattended in this area.

- **Boundaries**: Use baby gates to close off areas such as stairwells and bedrooms to keep your dog from accessing them. We will learn how to reinforce these rules later.

Above all just use common sense when dog-proofing your home. If something looks like it could pose a threat to their wellbeing then deal with it. You can never be too careful.

"A dog will teach you unconditional love. If you can have that in your life, things won't be too bad."

Robert Wagner

CHAPTER 2

THINGS YOU'LL NEED

Now your home is dog-proof, here are a few things you will find handy. You can download a more complete guide at the back of this book.

SUPER IMPORTANT: Do not purchase so called 'training aids' such as spiked or electric collars. These will cause serious distress to your dog and completely ruin your relationship with them.

* **Collar**: There is a wide variety available but something flat and adjustable with a quick-release system is a good place to start for a growing dog.

* **Leash**: Invest in a good quality leash which is compatible with the collar. Avoid extendable leashes at all costs as these cause the dog to pick up bad habits during walks.

* **Treats**: Stock up on small, dry treats to reward your dog for successes during training. Talk to a pet care specialist about the right treats for your particular dog and make sure you don't overfeed them.

- **Crate or Bed**: Dogs need a place to call their own so getting a nice crate or bed is very important. They are likely to chew on and scratch at and generally mess up their little home so be sure to buy something durable.

  A crate should be big enough for the dog to stand and stretch out in, but not so large that they end up using one section for sleeping and the other as a toilet area

- **Training Pads**: These are useful during toilet training and much more effective than laying down newspaper or cardboard.

- **Clicker**: Some people like to use these as a training aid. It is not necessary and is really up to you to decide, but if you do purchase one be sure to use it properly and regularly.

- **Whistle**: Similar to a clicker, this is not essential kit but if you struggle to project your voice and would like to train your dog to respond to a whistle then pick up a decent training whistle rather than cheap alternatives.

- **Toys**: Dogs love to play, so get a couple of durable toys for them to chew on. These are also useful for preventing them from chewing on your personal possessions!

It's a good idea to get a puzzle toy too, as these can occupy the dog for longer periods of time which will become useful later. Just make sure they won't fall apart as you don't want them swallowing the pieces.

- **Patience**: You can't buy it in the shops but you're going to need it by the bucket load! Raising a dog is as big a commitment as parenthood in the early days, so be prepared for any eventuality and never take your frustrations out on your new friend.

"Everything I know, I learned from dogs."

Nora Roberts

CHAPTER 3

YOUR DOG'S TIMELINE

If you're reading this book then you may have picked up your furry little friend by now, but if you haven't then this part is especially important. If they are home already, read on anyway to understand what they got up to whilst waiting for you to come along.

SUPER IMPORTANT: Most people don't take a dog home until it is at least 8-12 weeks old, so the environment it has been raised in until that point plays a major part in its development.

It is absolutely essential that you get your dog from a reputable place. Do your research and always visit the premises up front to check on the standards of the environment. You can also request pedigree information to find out more about the dog's genetics.

Avoid seedy advertisements from people who are churning out dogs for money at all costs and only consider a proper home where the dogs have the best possible care. If alarm bells ring then please do not be tempted to conduct a rescue mission; you will be much better off reporting any unscrupulous activity to the relevant authorities and letting them take care of it.

Now we've cleared that up, here's a quick rundown on how dogs develop from the time they are born to when people tend to take them home.

DAYS 0-7

Puppies are born blind and deaf, but can smell well enough to locate their mother for warmth and nourishment.

During this period they will sleep around 90% of the time, getting up only to eat or eliminate (that's pee and poop to you and me) and will need physical assistance with this task for a while.

DAYS 7-14

During the second week a puppy's eyes and ears begin to open. They also attempt to stand up, and invariably fail in an adorable fashion.

DAYS 14-21

Puppies begin to crawl around, walk (wobbly) and explore surroundings. Eyes start focusing and milk teeth (baby incisors or front teeth) emerge. They will also start feeling out objects with their paws at this point.

Towards the end of this week the critical socialization period begins where the puppy will need to interact with its littermates as well as humans.

Here weaning also begins for bigger puppies and proper walking and playing will start to take place. Tails will wag and most pups will also be able to eliminate without assistance (yay!)

DAYS 21-28

Puppies can begin to take formula from a bowl. Eye color changes and the puppy will start to groom itself. At the end of this period a full set of baby teeth should have come through, and the puppy can begin eating soft food.

WEEKS 4-5

Basic housetraining typically begins around this time and the puppy will receive gentle human handling.

Weeks 5-7

Puppies begin greeting littermates with nose and tail sniffing, and forming proper relationships with people. They will also be on dry food by the end of this period.

Weeks 7-10

He or she should have a full set of puppy teeth by now. Some pups may be sprayed or neutered at this point. By week 8 it is common for many puppies to be rehomed.

Weeks 10-12

Puppies are normally fully weaned by now. This is also a crucial 'fear imprint' period where traumatic events can scar a dog for life. This is why it is so important that they are raised well by the breeder.

Weeks 12 - 16

Your puppy will begin chasing things and shortly enter adolescence. Most people will have their puppy home by now.

This is also a time of intense competition between littermates as the puppy nears full development and tries to figure out who is boss.

4-8 MONTHS

Your puppy's adult teeth will begin growing in as they enter the equivalent of a 'teenager' phase in the dog world. This is when training can generally be scaled up from the bare essentials to slightly more advanced work.

They may show signs of independence and even appear to forget basic training, but with a consistent schedule you will make it through any bumps in the road.

6-14 MONTHS

Dogs experience hormonal changes and growth spurts during this period which may result in some strange behavior.

They may appear frightened of new situations, become a little territorial or reactive. This is perfectly normal and you will learn how to sail through this with strong leadership.

18-24 MONTHS

This is the 'young adult' stage where similar behavior to that during months 6-14 may resurface or carry over. Hopefully your dog will be well along the training line by now so there should not be too many surprises, but if you are starting fresh with a dog older than this then you will still be able to get them on track using the methods in this book.

Just remember, if you know where your dog came from and was raised then you will have a better idea of their behavioral traits. If you pick them up at random then be patient as you discover and deal with any of the above character quirks.

CHAPTER 4

TRAINING SCHEDULE

SUPER IMPORTANT: If you are in a bad mood, postpone training. You are likely to become more frustrated than usual and there's a chance you may take this out on your dog. Only train when you feel you have the positive mind frame and patience to do so.

THE SCHEDULE

It's best to keep training sessions short and sweet. For example, it's better to do three to six 5-10 minute sessions throughout the day than spend an hour on one. Dogs have a short attention span and often lose concentration quickly so you want to embed new knowledge while you have their full attention.

Only you will know your own schedule, but generally speaking you should be dedicating time to training every day. Around 3-6 sessions per day is a good place to start depending on your dog's age and current level of training.

You'll find a blank schedule available to download at the end of this book. If possible, talk to the breeder or previous owner of your dog and use the information provided to fill it out.

If you're starting from scratch then begin with the simple stuff. Write down the time and what you have accomplished each day e.g. '09:00 | Sit training (10 mins)' and use the notes section to keep track of progress, highlighting where your dog is doing well and where they need to improve.

Once your dog is completely comfortable with a certain task – and they really must nail it – you can add something new into their schedule. Be sure to keep hold of the old copies of the schedule in a folder somewhere as training can take months and you may want to refer back to them.

Plan ahead so you can make the most of the time you have together. If possible, take some extra time off during the first week or so as this is when your dog needs you most.

Remember, every interaction with your dog will have an influence on them so do not 'switch off' around them just because you're not doing drills A police officer must uphold the law even when he's not on duty, just as you must maintain the standards and boundaries you have set for your dog in day-to-day life.

REALISTIC EXPECTATIONS

Don't expect to read a chapter of this book, go away and practice it and then be able to move onto the next section. Training a dog is similar to educating a child in that it requires patience, commitment and constant practice.

Instead of trying to work through each step of this book once, think of it as a resource which is here to help you on an ongoing journey. Have it open each day to keep you moving in the right direction and I promise that you will see progress.

Tip: Finish every training session with an exercise you know your dog can perform. By ending on a positive note you will both go away happier and look forward to the next session.

"The only creatures that are evolved enough to convey pure love are dogs and infants."

Johnny Depp

CHAPTER 5

BECOMING PACK LEADER

This is arguably the most important aspect of dog training, so please soak up every single word and remember to uphold your status at all times.

From the moment a puppy is born its mother begins the training process. She dictates when food is available, gives permission to play, enforces the boundaries of physical contact, sets borders for exploration and so on.

She is calm, assertive and unwavering in her authority and this enables her to keep her entire litter in order. Now, think about what happens when you take a dog out of that environment and away from its mother.

Effectively you open up a vacancy for pack leader and, if left unfilled, your dog will go off the rails without the constant guidance it needs. It is up to you to step into this position and firmly establish yourself as pack leader.

Follow these guidelines to ensure your dog understands and respects your authority at all times:

- **Body language**: Be calm and assertive whenever you interact with your dog. You must exude confidence in order to gain respect.

- **Boundaries**: Limits exist both in terms of physical environments and behavior. It is essential to set these early on and maintain them throughout training.

- **Control**: Dogs need constant reminders of who is in control. For example, having them sit and remain calm before giving them dinner will teach them this form of respect. We will learn such techniques later.

- **Consistency**: You will hear it said many times over because it is essential to remember this point. You cannot be a part-time pack leader so take your role seriously and remember to live it every day.

CHAPTER 6

HOW DOGS LEARN

Dogs, like humans, come preloaded with genetic instincts. These take care of survival as far as eating, drinking, sleeping etc. goes but they can also come with some other inbuilt character traits.

If a dog is bred for retrieving then it will demonstrate tendencies to do so and will therefore be easier to train for this practice.

Since dogs don't tend to be bred simply for sitting down or taking treats nicely from your hand, these are behaviors that you have to imprint through the art of positive reinforcement training.

In a nutshell this means rewarding your dog for good behavior so that it makes a positive association with said behavior and repeats it.

It also means absolutely never resorting to physical punishment or verbal scolding as this will not only destroy any chance of a loving, respectful relationship with your dog but they simply won't learn from it either.

Positive reinforcement paired with consistent training is the only way to imprint long-term habits in a dog's brain.

Essentially the cycle works as follows:

- **Cue**: This is you giving a command such as raising your hand and saying 'sit'.

- **Habit**: This is your dog performing the action, in this case sitting down.

- **Reward**: This is where you provide a reward such as a small food treat.

Over time as your dog enters the 'maintenance' stage of training you will be able to scale down both the cues and rewards in order to achieve the desired habit.

For example, once your dog is completely obedient to the 'sit' command, you will simply be able to raise your hand without speaking and they will recognize the cue and obey the command.

Where you would once have relied on food treats every time, you could then occasionally substitute them for simple praise and affection.

This book will guide you through essential obedience training with easy to follow drills. The importance of regular practice and consistent behavior from you cannot be overstated here.

Your dog's future depends on your commitment to his or her training. Give them the life they deserve, starting from day one.

"Dogs don't rationalize. They don't hold anything against a person. They don't see the outside of a human, but the inside of a human."

Cesar Milan

Chapter 7

Your Dog's First Day Home

So you just got your dog home and your overwhelming instinct is to invite family, friends, neighbors, colleagues, neighbors of colleagues and everyone on your Facebook friends list to come over and play with the little bundle of joy.

I don't want to deprive you of this indulgence, but what you do now is going to play a huge part in how your dog settles in to its new home, so please keep the below in mind before going all gooey!

When You Get Home

Leaving mum, dad, brothers, sisters and beloved humans behind and moving to a new home can be an exhausting and traumatic experience for a dog, so it is essential to make the transition as smooth as possible.

SUPER IMPORTANT: Hopefully you've already equipped your house with everything he or she will need. If you haven't, please revisit chapter 1 and make sure everything is in order.

Tip: Pick up your dog on a quiet week when you know you haven't got much else to do as you will need to pay them extra special attention during this period.

Now, the first port of call when you get home is to go straight to the designated toilet area. Your dog may be very excitable and might not be able to hold it in, so take them to this place before anything else and make a habit of doing so regularly.

Keep a close eye on them and make sure they go before bringing them back indoors. They might have a few accidents later on but this is to be expected and we'll cover the solution shortly.

SHOWING YOUR DOG AROUND

Dogs are incredibly inquisitive and the first thing they are going to want to do is explore their new environment. Don't drag them around the entire house as this may be overwhelming; instead let them explore the main living area under close supervision.

Next up, familiarize them with the location of their food and water. Do not be tempted to bring these to the dog as they must learn to associate this place with eating and drinking, just as they will learn to eliminate in the designated toilet area later.

They probably won't need a full meal at this point so one or two treats will be enough for them to make the initial association.

After this first introduction your dog may need a nap, especially if young. Don't keep them awake for your own self-satisfaction; let them rest and work around their schedule.

MEETING FAMILY, FRIENDS & OTHER PETS

Socializing is a hugely important part of your dog's development, but just like us humans not all of them take to it straight away. Some will be outgoing, others introverted and nervous. For this reason you should not overwhelm your dog with visitors before you really know their character.

Start off by introducing immediate family only. Of course, I don't expect you to shut other pets away; quite the opposite in fact since they qualify as family too.

You should pay extra special attention to resident dogs or cats and give them lots of praise and affection to ensure they don't feel forgotten about or competitive when a new arrival enters the scene.

Generally speaking, though, keep groups small and ease off if you see signs of your dog becoming intimidated or scared.

If you have young children make sure they act calmly around the dog; running around screaming with excitement can cause dogs distress. Kids will often react badly to being scratched or bitten too so it's a good idea to let them watch you during training so they learn the proper way to interact with him or her.

Bear in mind that with every meeting your dog is learning how to behave around people, so start as you mean to go on by ensuring you set a calming environment as opposed to one which will work them into a frenzy.

This is not to say that you can't play with your dog; just be sure to keep those groups small and let them take the initiative. Expect to be scratched and bitten and yapped at and possibly peed on depending on your dog's age – we'll cover how to deal with these things soon.

SEPARATION ANXIETY

When a dog is separated from its first family and taken to a new home they may howl and whine. Even once settled in they sometimes continue to do so when left alone.

This is completely normal and happens as a result of their instinctive fear that they are being abandoned by their pack. By howling and whining they are effectively sounding the alarm so that someone will come to the rescue.

Now, no matter how heart wrenching this is, coming to the rescue is exactly what you should not make a habit of doing.

The first course of action here is to get your dog accustomed to being left alone. Even when you are home it is good practice to spend some time apart so that when you do leave the house they don't become stressed or scared.

Here's a step-by-step drill to deal with separation anxiety:

1. Start by settling your dog down in his or her own area, bed or crate.

2. Offer a small treat before departing for a short while. If he or she cries out do not be tempted to rush back and offer reassurance as this will train them to believe they can get your attention by howling or whining.

3. Wait until they quiet down and then go back to offer a reward for this good behavior. If your dog continues to cry out then sternly tell them 'no!' and wait until they have stopped to interact with them again.

4. Gradually increase the time you leave them alone until they are comfortable with it.

If a dog howls or whines incessantly when left alone then they probably aren't comfortable in their surroundings yet, so spend a bit of extra time getting them accustomed to it by socializing with them there throughout the day. Be sure to offer plenty of praise and affection as well as the odd treat while doing so.

Tip: Place a puzzle toy with a treat stuffed inside into your dog's confinement area. This will teach them to associate this place with fun and food while also distracting them from the fact that you may have left them alone.

Please note that if your dog howls or whines for prolonged periods or at strange times despite regular training then it may not be due to separation anxiety. In these cases it is always best to seek advice from a veterinarian to ensure there is no underlying issue.

CHAPTER 8

TRAINING WORDS & TONALITY

Once your dog is settled in you can begin training immediately, starting by establishing your key training vocabulary.

Believe it or not dogs can learn words. Or, more accurately, they can learn to associate that noise coming out of the big tall human's mouth with a certain behavior or activity. Two words in particular are essential early on.

SUPER IMPORTANT: Use the appropriate tonality when communicating with your dog. Be clear and stern when they do something wrong, and say it with an encouraging smile when they've achieved something positive.

No

It can be difficult to tell a dog off (darn their cuteness!) but it is absolutely necessary in order to establish certain boundaries. Being clear about this early on will help your dog learn right from wrong before they can cause any real damage!

When your dog steps out of line use 'no!' immediately afterwards. If you are scratched or bitten whilst playing, stop immediately and say 'no!' If your dog eliminates on your new shoes, show him or her the shoes and repeat 'no!' Remember, no physical punishment or scolding, ever.

The beauty of this word is that once it is learnt you can use it *before* your dog misbehaves. So, if you see them creeping up to another pair of shoes with a mischievous look on their face, a simple and stern 'no!' will remind them not to go any further.

After a while you will find you very rarely need to use this word, as your dog is smart and intuitive and will remember right from wrong. Next up is a word you'll enjoy using much more.

GOOD

Training a dog is not just about telling them when they've been naughty. In fact, that is secondary to letting them know when they've done well.

A simple 'good boy' or 'good girl' each time your dog does something right – or does not do something wrong – will rapidly speed up the rate of learning and make everyone feel warm and fuzzy inside.

Tip: Dogs, especially when young, can be just as ignorant as teenagers at times. If they have their head turned or are walking off when you are trying to communicate, be sure to get back into their direct line of sight and make eye contact before repeating yourself.

Remember, you are the pack leader and your dog has to learn to respect you from day one.

"Happiness is a warm puppy."

Charles M. Schulz

Chapter 9

Body Language

Dogs will learn to respond to your body language as well as the spoken word. Like words, this can be broken down into two basic variations.

Hostility

If your dog misbehaves you can let him or her know by withholding affection immediately. For example, if you are playing and they bite you, withdraw your hands straight away. If he or she has a habit of jumping up at you, turn your back to teach that this is not acceptable.

This can be tough to do at times but always remember that it is your responsibility to raise them right, and that if you don't do it now then any bad behavioral traits will be a lot worse when they are older, bigger and stronger.

Positivity

Here's the one you'll enjoy again! When your dog shows signs of behavioral improvement or obeys a command, be welcoming in your body language and invite them towards you to receive your affection.

For example, if they come to you when called, pet them so they know they have done well.

Tip: Combine body language, words and tonality to make it clear every time your dog has done something right or wrong.

CHAPTER 10

HOUSEBREAKING / TOILET TRAINING

The amount of toilet training required will depend largely on your dog's age. We will assume for the sake of covering all bases that you need to start from square one.

If your dog is housebroken already then you will still likely want to teach them the appropriate spots to go outdoors, so follow the below guidelines.

Tip: You and I once crawled the floors of our family homes leaking from all orifices, completely oblivious to the consequences. Remember that we all had to learn once and be patient with your dog during this phase.

Now, don't even go thinking about doggy diapers. Just don't. If you want to minimize the damage done to your home then laying training pads in places where your dog takes to going should be sufficient to soak up most spillages – more on how to use those later.

Setting a Designated Area

As with all learning processes consistency is key if you want your dog to understand the appropriate place to eliminate. Choose a particular area, preferably a corner of the back yard where there is little chance of anybody stepping in it.

If you keep moving this around your dog will simply never learn where it is supposed to go, so stick to the designated area religiously once established.

If you have a young dog or puppy then you can expect them to go just about anywhere during the early days. Take them to the general area each time anyway; eventually they will go there without needing any guidance from you.

Tip: If possible, ask the previous owner about your dog's toilet habits. They may have already established a routine which you will need to work with.

Toilet Schedule

Puppies normally need to eliminate as soon as they wake up, 15 minutes or so after eating (this stimulates their digestive system) and generally every 30-45 minute period of time when they have been awake and active. They'll also need to empty the tank just before bedtime and in many cases during the middle of the night, too.

Knowing this allows you to preempt and even avoid a lot of accidents by taking them to the designated toilet area at the aforementioned intervals every single day. Keeping a diary of your dog's last meal, drink and toilet time is a very effective way of minimizing accidents and ensuring your friend settles into a routine as fast as possible.

Older dogs can wait a little longer, although it will very much depend on them as an individual. The trick is again to keep note of their habits early on and establish a schedule.

For example, if you keep a diary for one week and find that your dog has eliminated 28 times, that would mean you should be letting them out 4-5 times per day.

This is very valuable information and I strongly encourage you to keep a log, if you'll pardon the pun. You'll find a blank toilet diary available for download at the back of this book, simply pin it up on the wall and get into the habit of using it every time.

After a while your dog should be able to tell you if it needs to go by sitting in the appropriate place, but you should still stick to the toilet schedule even if they have already been outdoors.

Rewarding Success

Each time your dog goes to the toilet in the designated area you should be sure to offer an extra special reward. Toilet training is the foundation of training in general so encouraging them to accomplish this as fast as possible will serve you well going forward.

SUPER IMPORTANT: Do not attempt to train your dog to obey a toilet schedule which suits you - this would cause unnecessary suffering. As they grow older dogs will be able to go longer between toilet breaks but for now you'll just have to work around them.

Training Pads

You will probably have some sort of protection laid down already but, if not, invest in some training pads as opposed to newspaper or cardboard. They are more absorbent and the scented varieties are actually designed to attract the dog to the pad when it needs to go. You will find an equipment guide at the back of this book with some suggestions.

While your dog is still young and unable to make it outside, lay a training pad as close as possible to the designated outdoor toilet area. For example, if you want to train your dog to use the back yard then place a pad just inside the doors so he or she gets used to running in that direction when it's time to go. Eventually you will be able to remove the pad entirely and the whole process will transition smoothly from indoors to outdoors.

ACCIDENTS

Even housetrained hounds can have accidents. Be patient with them and try to determine the cause of the leak, so to speak. There are a surprising number of factors which can lead to accidents. Look out for the below causes and treat them accordingly.

- **Marking Territory**: This is generally performed by dogs over 3 months of age, but if you notice yours urinating in small amounts on upright surfaces such as walls or sofas this could be the case. It is important to interrupt this immediately with a stern 'no!'

- **Separation Anxiety**: If you notice your dog repeatedly urinating or defecating in your absence then this could be the cause. Use the techniques learnt in chapter 1 to combat this behavior.

- **Submissive or excited:** Sometimes your dog will have an accident when greeted by people or during physical contact. Signs that your dog is being submissive including lowering of tail or head, averting of gaze, flattening of ears, sinking to the ground and rolling over etc. Signs of excitement will be more obvious!

Do not try to pacify your dog by petting or cuddling it during submissive or excited urination. Do not scold or punish them either, as these actions could encourage him or her to be even more submissive or excitable in an attempt to please you.

They key here is to build up your dog's confidence using the following techniques.

- Throw a couple of small treats or a toy in the direction of your dog as they come to greet you.

This distraction may take the edge off the situation for them.

- Ignore your dog when you first seem them after an absence. Wait until they are calm before interacting with them.

- When you greet them, do so calmly and avoid large groups.

- Avoid domineering body language such as bending over at the hips and looming over them from above. Instead, squat down at their level so they feel less intimidated.

- Avoid eye contact, instead looking to the side or at their tail.

- Pet your dog under the chin or chest rather than on top of his head or ears and do not offer this kind of affection if they roll over.

Using the training techniques shown later you can also teach your dog to sit when greeting people, effectively overriding the impulse to roll over or be submissive.

- **Medical Causes:** Persistent accidents could be down to a medical cause. If you have reason to rule out all of the above and consider your dog fully house trained then it is worth seeking further advice on this subject from a qualified veterinarian.

- **General Accidents:** If you catch your dog in the act of eliminating in the house all you have to do is follow these simple steps:

  1. Say 'no!' both with your voice and body language.

  2. Gently lead them to the designated toilet area.

  3. If they go there, offer praise and reward.

If you're not quick enough to catch them in time then I'm afraid there's not much you can do about that particular instance. Just clean it up, note down the time and make sure you get them outside at that hour the following day.

Remember, no scolding, no punishment, just this simple and effective drill. Accidents will happen but over time your dog will become accustomed to the appropriate times and places.

CHAPTER 11

CRATE TRAINING

We've already touched on basic crate training when discussing separation anxiety, but as this is a key part of your dog's daily life it is important to cover it in more detail.

A dog's crate is their home inside your home; a private area where they can escape the big wide world and get some rest. Initially, though, they may be reluctant to get inside and there will almost certainly be issues when they are left alone, especially if young.

THE RIGHT CRATE

First and foremost, it is important to invest in a crate which allows enough room for your dog to stand up and stretch in. The breed of your dog will determine how much they are going to grow but you might have to buy a size up or buy something extendable. Just make sure it's not so big that they end up using half for relaxing and the other half as a toilet area.

There are several different types of crate available but as a rule something durable and breathable is essential. If you opt for a wire crate you will need to get a cover to give it that 'den' feel which dogs love.

To finish off the crate, some sort of removable and washable bedding is ideal. This provides some much needed comfort and means you can clean the whole thing in the event of any accidents. You can find some suggestions in the equipment guide at the back of the book.

LOCATION

Your dog needs to get used to going to and from its crate so be sure to place it somewhere it can stay long-term. An ideal location is somewhere relatively high-traffic where people will come and go, but not so busy that your dog will be unable to get any peace and quiet, especially at nighttime. Kitchens or conservatories often make a good choice.

GETTING INSIDE

SUPER IMPORTANT: Do not force your dog into the crate or put them inside as a punishment. This is supposed to be a place of comfort, not a prison, and you want them to associate it with positive activities.

Here's a couple of ways to get your dog into the crate for the first time:

- Place food treats inside the crate and leave the door open to encourage them to head inside. Don't close the door or force them to stay inside; instead let them come and go freely for now.

- Giving your dog its meals in the crate is another great way of making an initial positive association.

- A puzzle or chew toy is a good substitute for food treats – throw one inside to encourage them to follow.

Remember to Shower your dog with praise and affection whilst in and around the crate. Engage in play with them there too, so they make a positive association with the place.

STAYING INSIDE

Once your dog is familiarized with coming and going from their crate freely you can encourage them to stay inside a little longer using the same techniques.

Offer an additional treat once they are inside the crate, continue to engage in play and offer lots of praise and affection.

CLOSING THE DOOR

Closing the crate door is a big step and should not be attempted until your dog is comfortable entering and staying inside.

Once this milestone has been reached use the following techniques to help your dog get used to this new development.

- If they are having their meals inside the crate, try closing the door until they have finished. The food will be their primary focus so they shouldn't be too bothered about the door being closed.

- When he or she is used to having the door closed whilst eating, start to leave it closed for a little longer and increase it in small increments. For example, leave it closed for 2 minutes after they have eaten and then, when they are comfortable with this increase it to 4 minutes and so on until you reach the 10 minute mark.

SUPER IMPORTANT: Remember not to let your dog out of the crate if they begin howling or crying. This will just teach them that they can control you by doing so, something which will become particularly irritating for you during the night!

BEING LEFT ALONE

The final stage of crate training is leaving your dog alone either while you are away. You cannot simply put them in there, close the door and wait for the whining to stop so make sure you've followed the above steps to gradually work them up to this point.

Here's a drill to get dogs used to settling down for longer periods of time:

1. Ensure that they are tired enough to stay in the crate without getting restless. Spend some time playing with them before encouraging them inside.

2. Once they're inside offer them a treat and spend a little time with them there. As usual, lots of praise and affection is useful to keep them happy.

3. Offer another small treat before departing for a short while. If he or she cries out do not rush back and offer reassurance as this will be counter-productive.

4. Wait until they quiet down and then go back to offer a reward for this good behavior. If your dog continues to cry out then sternly tell them 'quiet!'

and wait until they have stopped to interact with them again.

Just like before, increase the time left alone in small increments until they are completely comfortable there. In the early days it's a good idea to get up during the middle of the night and let your dog out to use the toilet if they are still young.

You may consider this an inconvenience but that's the commitment you took on when you brought the little guy or girl home so don't let them suffer just so you can get an extra 10 minutes of sleep.

Tip: Go through your regular routine when practicing this drill. For example, if you pick up your keys, put your coat on and then leave through the front door every day, role-play this scenario when leaving your dog along during training so your dog becomes accustomed to it.

CHAPTER 12

BEHAVIORAL TRAINING

This section deals with behavioral issues such as biting, scratching and barking. These differ from commands such as sitting and staying which we will cover next.

BITING

Puppies play and explore with their mouths so you can expect a lot of nipping early on. Older dogs can play in this manner too, so it's important to ensure they know the boundaries of what is acceptable.

There arc no 'drills' to deal with this behavior, but you can still combat it by reacting in the right way. Here's how:

- Provide a good quality toy to satisfy your dog's urge to bite and direct it somewhere safe.

- Avoid being too aggressive in games such as tug of war which encourage your dog to 'clamp' onto things. Learning the 'drop' command in the next chapter will also help here.

- When you are nipped or bitten during play, withhold affection immediately and declare 'no!'

- When your dog tries to mouth you, redirect his or her attention away from you with a small treat or toy.

Pawing

Dogs tap at you in the same way that a small child might to gain attention. As pack leader you must remember not to pander to their needs or they will develop this bad habit. Here's how to prevent it:

- Withdraw all attention when pawed. This means no eye, verbal or physical contact. Walk away for a short while if necessary to teach the dog that they cannot get your attention this way.

- If you are scratched during play then stop immediately and follow the above advice on withdrawing attention.

Barking

Dogs bark and to some extent you will have to deal with it. However, incessant yapping should not be tolerated and you will need to use your status as pack leader to make that clear.

Here's some tips on how to do just that:

- Understand why your dog is barking before working on it. This could be due to separation anxiety, the sounding of an alarm, insecurity or just because they feel like it.

  You will discover your dog's triggers over time and be able to act on them appropriately. The important thing is not to stop barking altogether, but to be able to stop it whenever you deem it inappropriate.

- Desensitize your dog to whatever is causing the barking by gradually introducing him or her to it more and more over time.

- Teach your dog to bark on demand with the 'speak' command later. This may sound counter-productive but it will enable you to add the 'quiet' command on afterwards. You will learn this technique later.

- Don't shout at your dog as this, to them, just sounds like you are joining in!

- Don't give affection or treats to pacify them as this is effectively a reward.

- Calmly and firmly try the 'quiet!' command. If successful, have your dog sit or perform another command in order to distract them from whatever was causing them to bark.

- If verbal commands can't cut through the noise try another form of distraction such as a loud clap, the dropping of something noisy or the slam of a cupboard door. Do this discretely as if it had nothing to do with you and it should be enough to 'snap' your dog out of its barking.

- If all else fails, simply withhold all interaction until your dog stops barking.

Chapter 13

Basic Commands

Now that you know the difference between behavioral and obedience training you can approach both accordingly. You should already be establishing and maintaining boundaries, and it's now time to introduce some basic command drills.

It is worth mentioning again that you cannot simply practice commands a few times and then expect to move on to the next one. The following drills may look absurdly simple and you may be wondering where the rest of the information is but the truth is this is all you need.

Simplicity and consistency are the keys to learning so practice the below little and often to cement the knowledge long-term.

Tip: Before giving a command, call your dog's name to get his or her attention to ensure you have been heard.

Sit

This is the most common starting point and a great foundation for further obedience training. Here's how it's done:

1. Take a treat and let your dog see it, then hold it above his or her head. If they try to jump up remember to remind them of the boundaries you have set.

2. Now use your free hand to *gently* encourage their bottom to the ground and at the same time give a firm command of 'sit'.

3. Make sure he or she has obliged, and then give the treat as a reward. Be sure to offer verbal praise in the form of 'good boy' or 'good girl' every time too.

When your dog has the hang of sitting with assistance you can be gentler when pushing their bottom to the ground.

You can then progress to simply moving your hand towards their backside when giving the command – if they are learning then they will respond to this gesture and, eventually, will not need it at all.

As your dog gets older they will not need to be rewarded with a treat every time, but giving them one every so often is a fair reward for remembering commands.

STAY

Once your dog has learnt to sit without assistance it is ready to learn to stay put.

As you move away they are likely to want to follow you – don't encourage this behavior as it could become frustrating or even dangerous. For example, you don't want them under your feet in the kitchen or following you onto the street when you leave the house.

Here's how to have your dog stay rooted once they've sat down:

1. Start by having them sit and reward them for doing so.

2. Now hold your empty hands up in a 'stop' gesture and give the clear command 'stay'.

3. Back away a short distance and keep your hands up, repeating the command if necessary. If he or she gets up and follows you – which they probably

will initially – say 'no' and lead them back to the sitting position to start the process all over again.

When your dog obeys this command, use the reward and praise techniques already learnt to ensure they know they've done well.

DOWN

Use this command to encourage your dog to lie on the ground. It's best to keep things simple here and avoid using the two word command 'lie down.'

Tip: Do not use 'down' as a disciplinary word when your dog jumps up at you or climbs on the furniture; this will become confusing when you train it to lie down later. Instead use 'off!' to combat this behavior.

1. Start with a treat half hidden in your hand and let your dog see it.

2. Give the 'sit' command but do not offer the treat immediately. Instead, lower your hand directly onto the ground and give the command 'down'.

3. The dog will likely scramble around your hand trying desperately to get at the treat, and this will normally lead them to get down on their belly.

When they do this and have settled down, give them the treat and praise them for a job well done.

If your dog isn't lying down then you can give gentle assistance with your free hand, repeating the command just as you did during training to sit. You don't need to be forceful here – your dog is weaker than you and will only need a little encouragement.

COME

I'm sure you're starting to see the natural progression of these commands, just as your friend will if trained little and often.

Bear in mind that this particular command can be very confusing for a young dog that is just learning to sit and stay, so it is important not to cross command boundaries here. Let them get the hang of one thing before jumping to the next and do not overload them with different commands all at once.

Here's the drill:

1. Start with having the dog sit and stay, and reward them accordingly.

2. Back away as normal and allow a couple of moments to elapse so you are sure they have understood.

3. When they have sat calmly for 10 seconds, switch your stopping hand gesture to a welcoming and encouraging movement and give the command 'come!'

   This should be all it takes to get them to come bounding over, but offer them a little extra encouragement if necessary. As with all successes, finish off with a reward.

4. Add the 'sit' command at the end of this drill as soon as possible to prevent jumping up.

   Tip: avoid the temptation to meet your dog halfway – they must learn to do the work themselves. You can slowly increase the distance over time and eventually perform this command when out of eyeshot altogether, but take it slow at first and ensure the knowledge is sinking in.

OFF

You may think your dog jumping up at you or other people is a show of affection, but that's not entirely true. Dogs can often be anxious and that causes them to bound towards people and seek comfort.

They jump up at you as a child would, seeking reassurance. By making a fuss, petting them or picking them up you will only encourage this behavior.

A puppy's mother would gently move them out of the way in order to create a clear boundary in cases such as this.

Here's a drill to replicate this yourself:

1. When you see your dog, do not give eye contact, speak to or physically come into contact with them until they are completely calm.

2. Once the dog is totally calm, try introducing the sit command if they are already familiar with it.

3. You may interact with your dog once you have clearly gained control of the situation.

Tip: teach your dog to sit whenever there is a knock at the door to prevent them racing up to visitors in the same way.

DROP

Your dog may occasionally latch onto things and not want to let go. Prevent this behavior with the following drill.

1. Offer your dog its favorite toy. You can even introduce the 'take it' command here to get them used to receiving things with permission.

2. Allow them to play for a while, and then have them sit in front of you with the toy.

3. Say 'drop' and at the same time offer a small food treat. Dogs always prefer food over fun so this should cause them to drop the toy.

LEAVE

Your dog's instincts will often take over, especially when it comes to food. Here's how to have them wait patiently for your approval.

1. Take a small food treat and place it in the palm of your hand, close to the gap between your thumb and index finger.

2. Close your fist and turn it over so the top of your hand is facing upwards.

3. Invite the dog to you and have it sit and sniff your hand. Once it finds the treat, state 'leave it' and wait for it to stop sniffing, nibbling or pawing momentarily and then open your hand to let them take the treat.

Tip: scale this drill up by asking your dog to 'leave it' as soon as you extend your hand towards them with the treat inside and making them wait longer to receive it. Eventually you will be able to begin this exercise with an open hand, or even with the treat on the floor.

GENTLY

If your dog has a habit of snatching you can prevent it by offering things in the correct manner. Use the below guidelines:

- Do not hold things in your fingertips as this makes it difficult for the dog to take.

- When your dog is comfortable with the 'leave' command and is sitting patiently waiting for a treat, introduce the 'gently' command to let them know they can take it. If they snatch, put your hand behind your back and state 'no!' before starting over.

SPEAK

Teaching your dog to bark on command can actually help prevent unwanted barking. It can also be useful for security purposes. Here's how:

1. Give your dog the 'speak' command and wait for him or her to bark two or three times.

2. Place a treat under their nose in a closed fist until they stop barking.

3. Once your dog has calmed down and is quiet, offer the treat.

Tip: Once your dog is taught to bark on demand, add the 'quiet' command before sticking the treat under his or her nose in order for them to make an association with the word.

PUTTING THE BASICS TOGETHER

Once your dog has mastered these techniques you can start putting them together. For example, when they have sat, have them stay. Once they've stayed put for a short time, have them come to you and then immediately command them to sit again.

Remember to keep the sessions short and productive and reward each success. If you become frustrated or the dog seems disinterested then call it quits and revisit the training a little later.

CHAPTER 14

USING A COLLAR AND LEASH

There are no hard and fast rules when it comes to introducing your dog to a collar and leash; every one of them responds differently but there are some steps you can take to ease them into the process.

CHOOSING THE RIGHT COLLAR

There's a wide variety of collars on the market and each have their pros, cons and uses, but one which I will categorically rule out as an option right now is the 'pinch' or 'prong' collar.

These barbaric devices are designed to cause dogs pain when they tug on a leash. As you know by now, we are all about kindness and reward-based training so steer well clear of these things as well as electrical shock collars.

Now, as far as options go, it's best to start off with something lightweight, flat and adjustable for a puppy or young dog. They are going to grow fast and you don't want to be shelling out for different sizes. Something with a quick release mechanism will also be useful for training.

INTRODUCING THE COLLAR

Wearing a collar is just as unnatural for a dog as it would be for a human, so don't simply shove it over his or her head and expect them to be ok with it. Instead, introduce the collar gradually during play and when giving treats so the dog learns to associate this strange new object with positives activities.

Remember that to your dog this probably just looks like another chew toy, but it is important to make it clear that this is not the case. If - well let's face it - *when* they try to bite or chew the collar, withdraw and tell them 'no!'

Allow them to nudge, sniff and lick it at first – this is how dogs get to know different objects – but don't let them be too rough.

When they are able to be near the collar without paying it too much special attention, reward them so they know to carry on this good behavior. You can then move onto the next step.

PUTTING THE COLLAR ON

Now that your dog is comfortable around the collar it's time to get them used to wearing it.

Tip: Unclip the collar for this training exercise – this will enable you to perform the process seamlessly.

1. Take a treat in one hand and wrap the collar around the wrist of the same hand but don't fasten the catch.

2. Close your fist so the dog can still see the treat. Move your hand towards their mouth and let them sniff the treat.

3. At the same time as opening your hand to let them take the treat, slip the collar down over your hand and around their neck, releasing it immediately afterwards.

Repeating this process little and often just gets them used to the feeling of putting the collar on. When they are comfortable with this, you can repeat the drill with a slight difference.

Instead of instantly releasing the collar, fasten it at the final step and leave it on for a few moments. Give treats, praise and affection immediately so they learn a positive association with this action.

Keep scaling this process up by leaving the collar on for a few seconds at first, then a few minutes, then a few hours until they are totally comfortable wearing it.

SUPER IMPORTANT: Always ensure you can comfortably fit two fingers between the collar and the dog's neck – any fewer and it is probably too tight and should be adjusted. At the same time, make sure it won't slide off over their head.

You should also keep a close eye on your dog when they begin exploring with the collar on – it could easily get stuck on something and you will need to be around to help them free if this happens.

NOW FOR THE LEASH

Once your dog is comfortable with the collar on you can introduce the leash in a similar way. Again, they are probably going to be baffled by this fascinating new object, so let them get to know it slowly.

It's good practice to start this exercise with the collar on, and simply let your dog sniff out the leash as they did with the collar before.

If it helps, bunch up some of the leash in your hand so they can only see a little bit at first. This will prevent them from trying to follow the entire length which could lead to a loss of concentration.

Again, reward him or her with treats, play, praise and affection when they behave well and give them a gentle reminder if they become a bit too physical.

1. Just as you did with the collar, attach the leash whist offering a treat and remove it quickly afterwards.

2. Gradually increase the amount of time the leash is left on until your dog is completely comfortable with it. Playing and socializing with them while the leash is on is a good way to distract them from the leash itself.

3. Finish this process by letting the dog walk around the immediate area so they become used to moving around with the leash on. Resist the urge to grab or pull on the leash to prevent them from going too far; instead rely on the techniques and commands already learnt and simply get them used to wearing the leash.

It's worth mentioning again that you should never leave any dog, young or old, alone with a collar or leash attached as it could very easily get trapped on something.

PICKING UP THE OTHER END

Now that your dog is comfortable with their collar and leash you might be tempted to head outdoors and show them off, and I hate to be captain killjoy but you probably know what is coming!

Before you can take a dog for a walk outdoors you need to get them used to walking on the leash in an environment they are familiar with. The big bad world offers countless distractions and they are likely to try to bolt off anywhere and everywhere.

This may cause them to pull forcefully on the leash, causing damage to their throats as well as forming bad habits which will be much harder to break later down the line.

So, as you have done with everything else so far, start off slow and steady. Your dog should already be familiarized with little walks around the house while the collar and leash are attached, so you can naturally progress this activity as follows:

SUPER IMPORTANT: Place the hand loop around your wrist and hold the leash in your right hand, letting it run across your body and using your left hand to grab it again near your left pocket. This will keep the dog close and encourage them to walk in the heel position – more on that soon.

1. Once you have the leash on and have offered a reward, pick up the other end and make sure to keep it slack.

2. Follow the dog around the first few times just to get them used to the leash.

3. Going forward use the 'come' technique already learnt to encourage him or her to follow you around the immediate area.

Avoid jerking the leash or dragging them around as this will not teach them anything other than to hate the whole process which will make future walks a misery.

Remember to concentrate on voice, body language and reward-based feedback. Your pup will learn much faster this way and it will be a more enjoyable experience for you both.

Tip: When the dog does tug on the leash, simply stand still. This sends a clear message that when they start pulling, you stop walking. Do not pull back; just stand firm and encourage them back to you so you can start the process again.

Heel on The Leash

We've slowly been working our way up to teaching your dog to enjoy walking on the leash and hopefully they are beginning to pick it up. Do remember, though, that all individuals are different and some might need a little extra work here and there.

Once he or she is behaving well on the leash inside the house you can begin to incorporate the 'heel' command. Note that we are still operating indoors for this exercise or at the very least in a secure and enclosed place – we'll get outside soon I promise!

1. Start by putting on the leash as normal and hold it in the correct position. Have the dog start seated just behind your left heel, then use the command 'heel' and begin to walk. The chances are that they are going to bolt off as soon as you start walking but as always we have a secret weapon which can bring them back into position; treats!

2. Have a pocketful of little food snacks handy and hold one just below your left hip to encourage them into position. They are likely to jump up and grab it at first but do not discipline them for this as it could be confusing. Instead, just wait for them to calm down before offering the reward.

3. If and when your dog wanders over to your right side continue walking but withhold the treats. Look over your left shoulder; say 'heel' and hold a treat in the usual place to encourage them back around. Be extra generous with your praise when they move back into the heel position from somewhere else.

As with all exercises you can incorporate other steps into the heel command once your dog has a good grasp on it. For example, when they come to heel, have them sit for another treat and lay down for another.

Note that this is quite an advanced command so expect to spend a little more time on this and be patient with your pet throughout.

"Dogs are not our whole life, but they make our lives whole."

Roger A. Caras

CHAPTER 15

GOING OUTDOORS

Now you have clearly established yourself as the pack leader and have taught your growing dog basic boundaries and commands, you can feel secure in taking them outdoors.

SUPER IMPORTANT: It is essential to ensure your dog has received all necessary vaccinations before taking them outside. If you are unsure then speak to a veterinarian; it is better to be safe than sorry.

Start off with a familiar and secure area such as the yard and practice your leash training drills there. When your dog shows signs of understanding that they are expected to behave both indoors and out, you can make their world a little bigger by walking them around the neighborhood.

EXPLORING NEW PLACES

The local area may seem small to you but by taking your dog even a few minutes away you are turning their world upside down. Don't be surprised if they seem a little slow on the uptake out here – they are trying to take a lot of new information in and you will need to be patient with them. Explore smaller, quieter areas at first and make sure he or she is comfortable before extending the walks.

You will no doubt have to deal with toilet duties while out and about. Unfortunately I haven't come up with a way of training dogs to clean up after themselves yet so you'll just have to make sure you have a few bags handy!

GREETING STRANGERS

Unless you live in a particularly secluded area you are likely to bump into other people when you go outside. This is a good thing as socialization is a pivotal part of your dog's development and will help them learn how to behave around new people.

Even though they may be accustomed to some folk already it is important to remember that each new person is completely alien to them, so bear in mind the techniques learnt in chapter 4 when it comes to making introductions.

Tip: Try to avoid extremely busy places and events until your dog is a little older as this may cause them distress and hinder their development.

When you inevitably do bump into someone they are likely to be drawn to your dog like a moth to a flame and some people won't think twice before swooping in to make a fuss of them.

Never force a dog into approaching strangers if they appear shy; instead allow them to observe from a distance and move closer if and when they are ready. As always, gentle encouragement and rewards for being brave are the way to go here.

If your dog isn't ready to interact simply apologize to the other person and explain that he or she is still a little shy. If they are a dog owner – or even a parent – they will understand!

MEETING OTHER DOGS

When you cross paths with another dog walker the chances of them stopping go from likely to definite because the dog will make the decision for them. Canines are inquisitive and will always go about their own greeting rituals when they meet.

Treat this scenario just as you would with meeting a new person; let your dog take the initiative and do not force them into anything they don't appear ready for. The other dog walker will likely see the signs anyway so they will completely understand if you have to cut the meeting short.

SUPER IMPORTANT: Keep a firm grip on the leash in situations like this. Your dog may be small but any sudden movements from another could cause them to bolt with surprising force and you do not want the leash to slip out of your hands.

It is also important to be vigilant in general as scraps can occur out of nowhere between dogs. If you notice tails stop wagging and go straight or if either dog begins to growl or show its teeth then encourage yours away.

CHAPTER 16

LEARNING NEVER STOPS

I started this book by mentioning how misleading the bogus the claims made by 7-day training programs and the like were, and it is important to bear this in mind once you've closed this book.

Please don't think that you can read this guide once, do each exercise a few times and then consider your dog trained. Consistency is the key to raising a good dog and you should continue to practice going forward in order to cement the knowledge long-term.

You can reduce the frequency of training as they get older, and you can also phase treats out and begin to focus more on praise and affection later on but you should never stop training entirely.

Always maintain your boundaries and consistently reward your dog for good behavior to ensure they don't slip back into bad habits.

Keep this guide handy to refresh your memory of the proper training techniques and refer back to specific drills.

Above all just be patient with them. I promise that with time, care and consistency they will grow up to be a well-mannered member of the family.

If you still have questions about the right way to raise a dog then check out the below FAQ's. In the meantime, I wish you and your new friend all the happiness in the world.

P.S. Don't forget, you can download my free training schedule and equipment guides at the back of this book.

FAQ's

Q: What vaccinations does my dog need?

A: You should find out from the breeder what shots have already been administered, and also talk to a vet about what is required. Generally, though, puppies are given DHLPP shots to protect against Distemper, Hepatitis, Leptospirosis, Parainfluenze and Parovirus at 7-8 weeks of age, and then twice again after 3 week intervals.

At the same time your dog will be vaccinated against the Coronavirus then, at about 16 weeks, will be given a Rabies shot. Annual boosters are then required going forward.

Q: What should I feed my dog?

A: This depends on the age, size and breed but you should generally choose something which offers a complete and balanced diet. Foods right in protein, fat, vitamins and minerals are essential for growing dogs so do not skimp on quality. Be sure to talk to a qualified professional to determine exactly what is right for your dog.

Q: When should I feed my dog?

A: Puppies tend to need feeding 3-4 times a day. Offer manageable meals instead of feeding them a larger quantity less often. Older dogs tend to need just breakfast and dinner. The exact amount will again depend on your dog's age, size and breed so it is always best to consult with a professional about your particular pet's needs.

Q: I can't break my dog's bad habits, what should I do?

A: Every dog is different and some will take more time to grasp things than others. Be patient and repeat the training drills little and often. If bad habits persist, try to hone in on the exact cause. Note down every misdemeanor including the time, location and possible cause. After a while you should be able to spot trends and deal with them accordingly.

Q: What are worms and how are they treated?

A: You may be able to detect worms in your dog's feces or even vomit. Also look out for a swollen stomach, a lifeless / rough coat of hair and a persistent cough. If you notice any of these symptoms take your dog to a vet to seek further advice or treatment. Do not purchase over-the-counter medication as there are several variations and only a professional will know which to prescribe.

Q: How does getting a new dog affect other pets?

A: Your resident pet may feel a bit left out when the new arrival comes and it is up to you and the whole family to make sure that is not the case. Pay extra special attention to your current pets when bringing a new one into the home. That way the resident cat or dog will learn a positive association with the new dog instead of feeling competitive.

Q: My dog destroys things when I am out, what can I do?

A: We covered separation anxiety earlier and this could be another symptom. Try using the methods discussed to train your dog to be comfortable in your absence. It also helps to give them something to do while you are out, such as a chew toy. You can also try leaving a radio on low volume to pacify them.

Q: I loved your book, where can I leave a review?

A: Well, thanks for asking! See the following page for a quick link to leave a review on Amazon and share the book with your friends.

Q: I'm still not sure exactly what stuff I need, can you help?

A: Sure, I've compiled a list of essential dog training equipment and accessories as well as some training schedule templates. See the following page to download them for free.

BONUS: FREE WEEKLY DOG TRAINING TEMPLATE, TOILET DIARY & TRAINING EQUIPMENT GUIDE

Training can be a daunting prospect and the last thing you need is to be unsure about your schedule or equipment.

To help you out during training I've put together a free bonus bundle including:

- Free Weekly Dog Training Schedule Template

- Training Equipment Guide

- Toilet Diary Template

Simply visit litomedia.com/dog-training to get yours!

LIKE THIS BOOK?

If you got value from this book, or from the free bonus guides, it would be wonderful if you could head over to your order history and leave a review to let me know. You can even include a picture of your dog ☺

P.S. Don't forget to tell your friends!